The Science of Living Things

What is a Cat?

Amanda Bishop & Bobbie Kalman

Crabtree Publishing Company

www.crabtreebooks.com

The Science of Living Things Series
A Bobbie Kalman Book

dedicated by Amanda Bishop
For Rian, the coolest cat I know

Editor-in-Chief
Bobbie Kalman

Editorial director
Niki Walker

Writing team
Amanda Bishop
Bobbie Kalman

Editor
Kathryn Smithyman

Copy editors
Molly Aloian
Rebecca Sjonger

Art director
Robert MacGregor

Design
Margaret Amy Reiach

Production coordinator
Heather Fitzpatrick

Photo researchers
Jaimie Nathan
Laura Hysert

Consultant
Patricia Loesche, Ph.D., Animal Behavior Program,
Department of Psychology, University of Washington

Photographs and reproductions
Frank S. Balthis: page 23
Erwin and Peggy Bauer: pages 8, 9 (top, bottom right), 13 (bottom),
   18 (bottom right), 19 (bottom), 21, 24, 25 (top)
© Steve Bloom/stevebloom.com: pages 4, 16
© Ian Coleman www.colemangallery.com: pages 30-31
Robert McCaw: page 27 (bottom left)
McDonald Wildlife Photography, Inc.: Joe McDonald: page 28
Allen Blake Sheldon: page 27 (top)
Tom Stack & Associates: Joe McDonald: page 29;
   Gary Milburn: pages 9 (bottom left), 25 (bottom right)
Michael Turco: page 17
Other images by Adobe Image Library, Corbis Images,
Digital Stock, and Digital Vision

Illustrations
Barbara Bedell: pages 5 (bottom), 6, 9
Tammy Everts: page 19
Margaret Amy Reiach: pages 5 (top), 11, 14, 18, 23, 28
Bonna Rouse: page 20

Digital prepress and printing
Worzalla Publishing Company

Crabtree Publishing Company
www.crabtreebooks.com   1-800-387-7650

PMB 16A	612 Welland Avenue	73 Lime Walk
350 Fifth Avenue	St. Catharines	Headington
Suite 3308	Ontario	Oxford
New York, NY	Canada	OX3 7AD
10118	L2M 5V6	United Kingdom

Cataloging-in-Publication Data
Bishop, Amanda
   What is a cat?/Amanda Bishop & Bobbie Kalman.
      p. cm. -- (The science of living things)
Includes index
Describes the different types of cats, the physiology, behavior, and
lifestyles of both wild and domestic cats, the relationship between
cats and their kittens, and cats that are in danger of extinction.
   ISBN 0-86505-990-X (RLB) -- ISBN 0-86505-967-5 (pbk.)
   1. Cats--Juvenile literature. [1. Cats.] I. Kalman, Bobbie. II. Title.
III. Series.
   SF445.7 .K35 2003
   599.75--dc21
                                                      LC 2002012122

Contents

What is a cat?

A cat is a **mammal**. Mammals are **warm-blooded** animals. Their bodies stay at about the same temperature, even when the temperature of their surroundings changes. Mammals have hair or fur all over their bodies.

All cats have fur—even the special hairless **breeds** of cats. Female mammals give birth to babies that **nurse**, or drink milk from their mothers' bodies for several months after birth.

Cats, cats, cats

There are all kinds of cats in the world! Most cats look similar because they all belong to the same family of animals, the family *Felidae*. Almost 40 different **species**, or types, of cats live in the wild. Cats are generally divided into two groups—big cats and little cats. Big cats have slightly different features and habits than those of little cats. Many little cats live in the wild, but **domestic**, or pet, cats are also part of the little cat group. All pet cats belong to one species called *Felis catus*. Within the species, however, there are about 80 breeds. Breeds differ in color, size, and other traits.

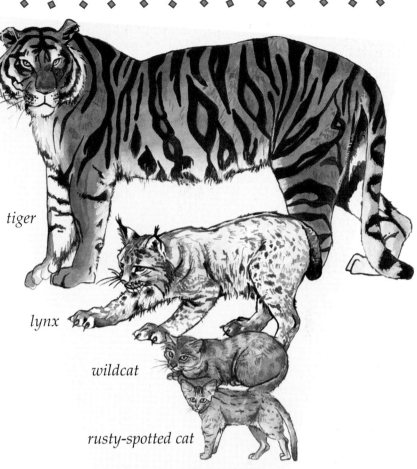

tiger

lynx

wildcat

rusty-spotted cat

The Siberian tiger is the largest cat in the world. It grows to 11 feet (3.3 m) in length, not including its tail! Compare its size to that of the rusty-spotted cat, which is only about one foot (30 cm) long. It is one of the world's smallest cats.

Cats way back

Scientists believe that cats are **descendants** of a prehistoric creature known as **Miacis**, shown right. This animal may also be an ancient relative of other **carnivores**, or hunters, such as dogs and bears.

Big cats

Lions, tigers, leopards, jaguars, pumas, and cheetahs are called big cats. All big cats naturally live in the wild. Tigers are the largest and longest of the big cats—and of all cats! Lions are a close second, followed by pumas (below), leopards, jaguars, cheetahs, and snow leopards. Big cats are strong runners and good hunters. Some big cat species make loud, rumbling roars that can be heard from great distances. Cats roar to warn other cats away from their territories and to frighten or even **stun** their prey. Not all big cats are able to roar, however. Pumas, cheetahs, and snow leopards have different vocal cords than other large cats have. To call loudly, they scream rather than roar.

Coats of many colors

Sometimes big cats are born with black coats. This coloring is called **melanistic**. It is most common among leopards, pumas, and jaguars, although some melanistic tigers have been seen. There are also "white" lions and Bengal tigers—their fur is much lighter than that of other lions and tigers.

Tigers

Tigers are the fiercest of the big cats. They are best known for their stripes, which are on their skin as well as on their fur. Most tigers have bold dark stripes on orange coats, but some people have seen tigers that have light stripes on black fur! In the last fifty years, three kinds of tigers have become extinct. There are only about 5,000 tigers left in the world today.

Cheetahs

Cheetahs are the fastest mammals on land. They are different from the other big cats. Their bodies are smaller— usually only three to five feet (1-1.5 m) long, not including their tails. Cheetahs are also the only cats that cannot pull in their claws. Their claws are always pushed out. Unlike the rest of the big cats, which usually hunt after dark, most cheetahs hunt during the day.

Little cats

There are all kinds of little cats! The colors and markings of many little cats look like those of the big cats, but their bodies and behaviors are different. Little cats do not roar as the big cats do, and they tend to groom themselves more often.

(left) Temminck's cat is also called the Asiatic golden cat. It has bold markings on its face.

The clouded leopard is more closely related to the little cats than it is to the leopard and snow leopard of the big cat group. Its voice box and coat markings are similar to those of other little cats.

Cat kin

Wildcats are the closest relatives of pet cats. Scientists believe that wildcats in Africa were the first cats to become pets. Ancient Egyptians tamed African wildcats thousands of years ago. Some people in Africa still keep wildcats as pets.

Black cats

Little cats are sometimes born with melanistic coloring. These two cats are both Geoffroy's cats. The cat on the left has common coloring, but the cat on the right is melanistic. Geoffroy's cat is about the same size as a domestic cat. It lives in the trees of South America.

A cat's body

Cats of different sizes and species have the same basic features. Their strong, graceful bodies are powerful and **agile**, or able to move quickly and easily. Agility allows cats to move in ways that other animals cannot. Cats can walk along narrow rails without losing their balance, and they can easily scramble up trees. Agility also helps cats land on their feet when they fall. Even if they fall upside down, cats are flexible enough to twist their bodies and get their feet underneath them before they reach the ground.

All cats, no matter how big or small, have more bones than you do! A cat has 230 bones in its skeleton, whereas you have only 206 bones.

Cats are **vertebrates**. All vertebrates have a backbone, or **spinal column**.

A cat uses its tail to keep its balance, especially while running.

Cats have tough pads on the bottom of their feet. These pads help them move quietly. All cats are good hunters, and their ability to move without making noise is especially useful while **stalking** and hunting.

Big mouth

Cat tongues are covered with coarse bumps called **papillae**. Cats use these bumps for tasting. They also use them to help groom their fur, to lap up water, and to clean meat off bones. The bigger the cat, the sharper the bumps!

Cats are carnivores. They have 30 sharp teeth that they use to bite prey and gnaw meat off bones. Cat jaws do not move from side to side, so they cannot grind food as human jaws can. Instead, cats tear off chunks of meat and swallow them whole.

A cat's fur coat may be long or short; dark or light; spotted, striped, or plain. The coat is made up of short **underfur** and long **guard hairs**. Underfur keeps the cat's body warm. Cats in cold climates have thick underfur to protect them from the cold weather. The long guard hairs keep the underfur dry. All cats groom their fur. They clean it with their claws, teeth, and rough tongues.

Out come the claws

A cat has claws on every paw. It keeps the claws inside its paws most of the time but pushes them out if it gets nervous. A cat uses its claws to climb trees, clean mud out of its fur, and defend itself. Cats like to **strop**, or drag, their claws by scraping them on trees (see page 28). Some pet cats also strop their claws on a scratching post—or on household furniture!

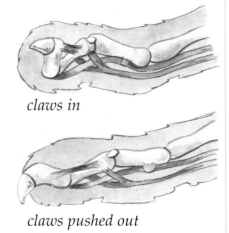

claws in

claws pushed out

Cat senses

All cats—even pets—are **predators**, or hunters. They have keen senses that help them detect **prey**, or animals to hunt. Even cats that are fed by people every day may hunt just because they are cats.

Cat's eyes

Cats have large eyes. Their **pupils** get bigger or smaller to let in more or less light. The pupils of little cats narrow to vertical slits in bright light, but big cats have pupils that appear more round.

Special layer

Cats have a special layer, called a **tapetum lucidum**, at the back of each eye. This layer collects every bit of light, even at night, and reflects it to help the cat see. The light that reflects off the tapetum lucidum sometimes gives a cat's eyes an eerie glow in the dark.

Many cats have dark markings in the fur around their eyes, which makes the eyes appear less round.

Can you feel it?

Whiskers are the long, sensitive hairs on a cat's head and face. They help the cat feel its way around when it cannot see well. If a cat can put its head through an opening without brushing its whiskers against the sides, it knows the rest of its body will fit, too.

Listen up!

Cats have an excellent sense of hearing. They pick up even tiny sounds with their ears. When a cat hears a strange noise, it points its ears toward the sound and listens carefully.

Sensitive snout

All animals, even humans, give off a scent. A cat uses its nose to detect the odors of other animals. It also uses an organ in the roof of its mouth that allows it to taste scent particles. The organ is called **Jacobsen's organ**. Your cat is using its Jacobsen's organ if it opens its mouth to make a **flehmen**, shown right.

Chatty cats!

scent glands

*When a cat rubs its face against your legs, it is using scent to communicate. A cat marks its **territory**, which includes people and objects, with scent from its scent glands.*

Pet cats meow to get attention from people—often because they want food or affection. Big cats such as tigers are able to meow only when they are kittens. Once they grow up, they roar just as their parents do!

Cats may not speak a language, but they can still communicate. They send messages to one another—and to us—using sounds such as purrs, hisses, and growls. They also use movements and **body language**, such as swishing tails and arched backs, to express themselves.

That sounds purr-fect

The most familiar cat sound is the purr. Cats purr when they feel friendly or at ease. Scientists believe that purring is also a soothing sound for cats. Sick cats sometimes purr to themselves. Kittens and their mothers purr while the babies nurse.

Grrrr-owling, yowling cats

Hisses, **caterwauls**, and roars are noises that cats make to show **aggression**. Cats hiss or make low growling sounds when they feel threatened. They caterwaul to make challenges, usually for the right to **mate** with a female. A roar is the scariest cat sound of all. When a big cat roars, its loud, rumbling call tells animals nearby that a hunt is starting!

Making it clear

Cats are very expressive animals, but their body language is sometimes difficult for humans to understand. For example, a cat that swishes its tail back and forth is probably irritated, but a cat that twitches its tail gently may be showing that it is friendly. Many people have observed different cats using the same behaviors to signal the same things, such as aggression or affection. People use these patterns of behavior to figure out what cats are "saying." Still, it is difficult to know the exact messages cats are sending.

When a cat looks you in the eye, it is showing that it trusts you. If your cat's eyes are slightly droopy, the cat is probably relaxed and happy.

"I'm warning you!"

This snow leopard looks as any cat does when it is ready for a fight. First, it bares its teeth and flattens its ears against its head. It then makes its hairs stand on end to make itself look bigger than it really is. Every hair in the cat's coat is attached to a muscle that allows the cat to move the hair. Finally, the cat crouches slightly on its rear legs— ready to leap into action!

Smitten with kittens

When a mother cat needs to move her cubs from danger, she carries them by their scruffs.

All cats start their lives as kittens. The babies of most big cats are called **cubs**. Whether they are cubs or kittens, baby cats need a lot of attention! The young are completely dependent on their mothers for the first few weeks of their lives.

A good mother

Almost all kittens are born in **litters** of two or more. The kittens are born blind. Their mother cleans them with her tongue and then helps them find the nipples on her underside so that they can begin to nurse on her milk.

Holding still

Cat mothers carry their kittens by the scruffs of their necks. All cats have a **reflex**, or automatic reaction, that stops them from moving when they are grabbed by the scruffs of their necks. Kittens that are carried by their scruffs cannot squirm.

Enough to eat

Most tigers in the wild hunt only about once a week, but a mother tiger hunts more often—especially when her babies are very small. She must hunt and eat more food in order to feed herself and her hungry cubs.

Forest cats

The jaguarundi has been called the "weasel cat" because its body is long like a weasel's body.

Cats that live in forests are excellent tree climbers, but many also spend a lot of time on the ground. Jaguars and ocelots live under the cover of forests. They hunt on the ground at night. Margays and kodkods almost always stay in the trees to hunt, sleep, and raise their young. Leopards hunt on the ground but carry their meals up into the trees and eat them there.

Ocelots and margays

The ocelot (left) and the margay (below) look alike, but ocelots are bigger. They live on the ground, whereas margays live in the trees. People **poach**, or illegally hunt, these cats for their beautiful coats. When it became illegal to hunt ocelots, poachers hunted margays instead. Now both cats are **rare**.

Margays are the only cats that can climb down trees after they have climbed up.

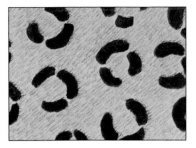

Leopards

Leopards are large spotted cats that spend much of their time alone. They sleep and eat in trees during the day and hunt at night.

Jaguars

Jaguars are jungle predators. They wait in trees for prey to pass below them on the ground. They then jump down and kill it by biting through its skull.

Grassland cats

Grasslands are areas where plenty of grass grows, but not many trees do. There is little shade to protect cats from the hot sun. Many grassland cats sleep most of the day and hunt at night when it is cooler.

Proud cats

Most cats live alone, but lions live in family groups called **prides**. A pride is made up of related lionesses, their cubs, and one to three adult males. Prides live and hunt together on large territories of land.

Shhhhh!

The serval, shown left, uses its big ears to listen for rodents. It can even hear them moving in underground burrows! The serval leaps high into the air to pounce on its prey or digs into a burrow with its long paws to catch a meal.

"Mind your own business!"

Unlike most grassland cats, cheetahs on the African **savannah** hunt during the day. Tour guides often bring buses and trucks close to the animals so that tourists on safari can catch a glimpse of cheetahs while they hunt. Unfortunately, the vehicles draw attention to the cheetahs, and the prey escapes before the hunt can start. King cheetahs, such as the one shown above, are a type of cheetah that tourists do not disturb because these rare cats hunt at night. King cheetahs also look slightly different from other cheetahs. They have more obvious **ruffs** on their necks, and the black spots on their backs are so thick that they appear to form a single stripe.

Desert cats

Deserts are places where very little rain falls. Life in the desert is tough for cats because water can be hard to find. There are only a few types of cats that can survive in this harsh **habitat**.

Most desert cats live along the edges of deserts but also spend time in nearby grasslands.

The caracal, shown above, is a desert hunter that leaps into the air to catch birds in midflight!

The caracal

The caracal is sometimes called a desert lynx. It is easy to spot because it has long tufts of hair on the tops of its ears. Its coat of short fur helps it stay cool in hot, dry surroundings. Like most desert cats, caracals hunt at night when the air is cooler.

Sandy claws

The sand cat is a small cat with a wide head and a ringed tail. Hair grows on the bottom of its feet to protect its paws from the hot sand. The sand cat spends the day in the cool shade of its burrow. Unless it is disturbed, it comes out only at night.

Like most desert cats, the sand cat (above) and the manul (below) have short legs and stocky bodies.

A bearded cat?

The manul, or Pallas's cat, lives in the cold deserts of Asia. Some manuls also live in grasslands and on mountainsides. A manul has thick fur that keeps it warm, even in very cold temperatures.

Mountain cats

Many cats live on rocky mountain slopes. Mountain cats are very agile, a trait that makes them excellent climbers.

They also have to be good jumpers—sometimes the only way to get from one cliff to another is by jumping!

Mountain cats such as this bobcat must maintain a good grip and keep their balance as they make their way up and down mountainsides.

Mountain spots

The snow leopard lives high up in the mountains of Asia, where the weather is usually cold. Its body is well suited to snow and low temperatures. It has long, thick fur to keep it warm and sturdy legs and wide paws to help it move through snow.

(right) The pampas cat of South America lives on mountains, on grasslands, and in forests. Its close relative, the mountain cat, lives only in the mountains. The mountain cat is rarely photographed because it lives at least 10,000 feet (3000 m) up the mountainside!

(below) The puma is also known as the mountain lion or cougar. It can live in all kinds of habitats, including mountainsides. It is the largest cat in North America.

Snow cats

Cats that live high on mountains or in northern areas live in cold temperatures for much of the year. To survive, these cats must stay warm and dry, even in snow. They must also find enough animals to hunt. The Siberian tiger, shown above, is the world's largest land predator. Its cold habitat is in southeastern Russia.

Bigfoot

There are four types of lynx. The one on the right is a Canadian lynx. The long guard hairs of its furry coat keep snow and ice away from its underfur and skin. This cat has big, broad paws to grip slippery surfaces.

Bob the cat

The bobcat is another type of lynx. It lives in North America. It is smaller than the other types of lynx and has different coloring. The bobcat often lives in snowy climates, but it can also live in deserts and on mountains.

Fascinating cat facts

Pet cats and wild cats have a lot in common. They have similar habits and **instincts**. The biggest difference between the two groups is that wild cats do not like people!

Scratchy cats and nail-biters

All cats strop the claws on their front paws. Stropping helps cats mark their territories. They leave their scent on trees or scratching posts as they drag their paws along them. Stropping also keeps claws in top shape. As a cat draws its claws along a rough surface, it pulls off the dull outer layer of the claws. There is a sharper claw underneath each old layer. To get rid of the outer layers on their back claws, cats nibble them off.

Never race with a cheetah!

Cheetahs can move faster than any other land animal— up to 60 miles (97 km) an hour! Lightweight bones, broad paws, and special leg muscles that are just for running, help the cheetah move. Big nostrils and large lungs allow plenty of oxygen into its body.

Hard to spot

The spots and stripes on a cat's coat are for **camouflage**, or blending in with the animal's surroundings. For example, the snow leopard above blends in with the rocks around it. Even the orange and black stripes of tigers are camouflage. Prey animals such as deer see green and orange as the same color, so when tigers stand in tall grass, deer do not see them.

Helping out

Believe it or not, cats and humans have similar **DNA**, or body chemistry. Like humans, cats suffer from many diseases. Some of these illnesses resemble human medical conditions. Scientists researching cures for human forms of diseases, such as leukemia and diabetes, have learned a lot by studying cats that are sick with the **feline** versions of the illnesses.

Cats in danger

There are all kinds of domestic cats in the world, but fewer and fewer cats are surviving in the wild. They are disappearing for many reasons, but the most common reason is the destruction of their habitats.

A home for cats

Every cat, especially if it is wild, needs a territory in which to live. The territory must be home to enough prey animals for the cat to hunt. As people settle in more areas, the wild habitats of all animals are reduced. Cats and other wild animals must live in smaller, more cramped territories and compete with one another for a smaller food supply. Cats in these areas may starve and die out if there is not enough prey.

How can you help?

Many people in the world want to protect wild cats. You can learn all about wild cats on the Internet. Find great information at www.5tigers.org. At the Race for the Big Cats web site, http://bigcats.care2.com, you can click on a big cat, and sponsors will donate money for its protection!

Glossary

Note: Boldfaced words that are defined in the book may not appear in the glossary.

body language Actions, motions, or behaviors that animals use to communicate

breed A variety of domestic cat

caterwaul A loud, high-pitched shriek

descendant An animal that is a distant relative of an ancient animal

domestic Describing an animal that lives with humans

DNA Short form for deoxyribonucleic acid, or molecules in cells that determine how living things will grow and develop

feline Describing something related to cats

flehmen A response to odor that allows a cat to draw scent particles in through its mouth

habitat The natural environment in which an animal lives

instinct Natural behavior that is not taught or learned

Jacobsen's organ An organ on the roof of a cat's mouth, used for tasting and smelling

litter A group of kittens or cubs to which a mother cat gives birth at the same time

mate To make babies

melanistic Describing skin or fur with naturally dark coloring

pupil The dark portion in the middle of the eye that regulates the amount of light that enters the eyeball

rare Uncommon; a species in danger of becoming extinct

ruff The collar of fur around a cat's neck

savannah A flat grassland

stalk To stealthily track or follow prey

strop To drag claws over a rough surface

stun To daze prey with a loud noise so that it cannot escape

territory An area in which an animal lives and hunts and which is defended by that animal

Index

1 2 3 4 5 6 7 8 9 0   Printed in the U.S.A.   2 1 0 9 8 7 6 5 4 3